Caterpillars to Butterflies

Bobbie Kalman

Crabtree Publishing Company

www.crabtreebooks.com

It's fun to learn about Baby Animals

Created by Bobbie Kalman

Dedicated by Samantha Crabtree
To Kaleigh and Scarlet,
May your futures be as bright and
beautiful as you are.

**Author and
Editor-in-Chief**
Bobbie Kalman

Editor
Kathy Middleton

Proofreader
Crystal Sikkens

Photo research
Bobbie Kalman
Crystal Sikkens

Design
Bobbie Kalman
Katherine Berti
Samantha Crabtree
(logo and front cover)

Production coordinator
Katherine Berti

Illustrations
Bonna Rouse: page 24
(eggs in life cycle)
Margaret Amy Salter:
pages 3, 15, 21, 23,
24 (molting)

Photographs
© Corel: page 11 (top right)
© Creatas: page 11 (bottom)
© Dreamstime.com: pages
5 (top right), 13 (bottom)
© Shutterstock.com:
All other images

Library and Archives Canada Cataloguing in Publication

Kalman, Bobbie, 1947-
   Caterpillars to butterflies / Bobbie Kalman.

(It's fun to learn about baby animals)
Includes index.
ISBN 978-0-7787-3955-5 (bound).--ISBN 978-0-7787-3974-6 (pbk.)

   1. Caterpillars--Juvenile literature. 2. Butterflies--Juvenile
literature. 3. Butterflies--Metamorphosis--Juvenile literature.
I. Title. II. Series.

QL544.2.K327 2008   j595.78'139   C2008-907344-4

Library of Congress Cataloging-in-Publication Data

Kalman, Bobbie.
   Caterpillars to butterflies / Bobbie Kalman.
      p. cm. -- (It's fun to learn about baby animals)
   Includes index.
   ISBN 978-0-7787-3974-6 (pbk. : alk. paper) -- ISBN 978-0-7787-3955-5
(reinforced library binding : alk. paper)
   1. Caterpillars--Juvenile literature. 2. Butterflies--Life cycles--Juvenile
literature. I. Title. II. Series.

QL544.2.K3513 2009
595.78'139--dc22
                                                 2008048644

Crabtree Publishing Company

www.crabtreebooks.com   1-800-387-7650

Printed in the U.S.A./012014/SN20131105

Published in Canada
Crabtree Publishing
616 Welland Ave.
St. Catharines, Ontario
L2M 5V6

Published in the United States
Crabtree Publishing
PMB 59051
350 Fifth Ave., 59th Floor
New York, NY 10118

Published in the United Kingdom
Crabtree Publishing
Maritime House
Basin Road North, Hove
BN41 1WR

Published in Australia
Crabtree Publishing
3 Charles Street
Coburg North
VIC, 3058

What is in this book?

Butterflies are insects

Butterflies are **insects**. An insect is a small animal with six legs. It has three body parts: the head, thorax, and abdomen. Butterflies also have two feelers called **antennae**. Some insects cannot fly, but butterflies have wings for flying.

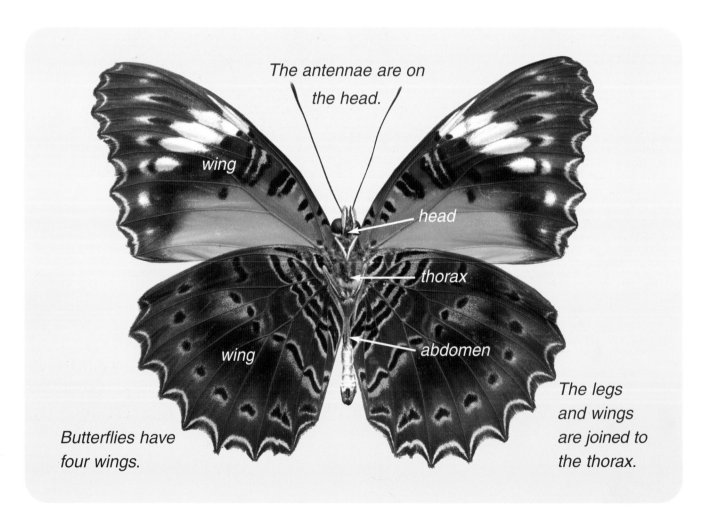

The antennae are on the head.

wing

head

thorax

wing

abdomen

Butterflies have four wings.

The legs and wings are joined to the thorax.

Butterflies have big eyes. They can see colors in flowers that we cannot see. Butterflies drink **nectar**. Nectar is a sweet liquid found in flowers. They suck up the nectar with a **proboscis**. A proboscis is like a long straw.

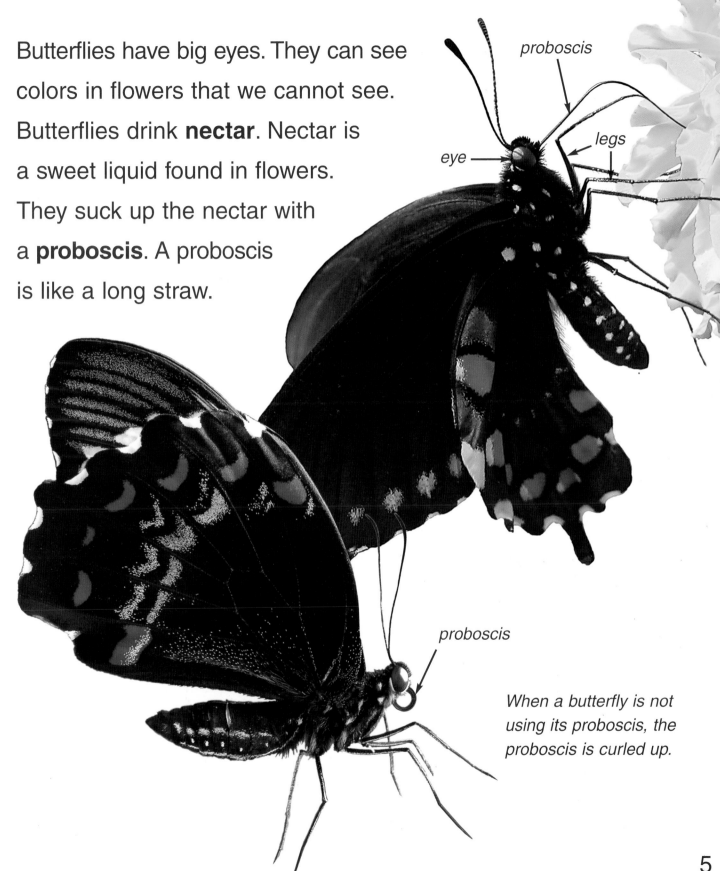

proboscis

eye

legs

proboscis

When a butterfly is not using its proboscis, the proboscis is curled up.

More about butterflies

There are many thousands of kinds of butterflies. Butterflies live all over the world, but they cannot live in very cold places. They are **cold-blooded** animals. Cold-blooded animals cannot make heat inside their bodies. Butterflies warm their bodies in the sun.

scales

A butterfly has four wings. Its wings are covered with **scales**. Scales give wings their color. Butterflies also have tiny hairs all over their bodies.

hairs

Butterflies or moths?

Moths are like butterflies. They are insects, too. Their lives are similar to the lives of butterflies. Butterflies and moths are different in a few ways, however. These pictures show how you can tell which is which.

Butterflies fold their wings above their bodies while they rest.

Butterflies have thin antennae with little clubs at the end.

club ➝

Butterflies fly during the day and sleep at night.

This butterfly is a peacock butterfly.

cecropia moth

How do moths look?

Moths are not as colorful as butterflies. They have thick, furry bodies. Their antennae do not have clubs like the antennae of butterflies. Moths look for food at night. They keep their wings open while they are resting.

atlas moth

9

From egg to adult

Butterflies are beautiful, but they did not always look that way. Butterflies start out inside eggs. Their bodies go through big changes. These changes are part of a **life cycle**. The life cycle of a butterfly has four **stages**, or parts. They are egg, larva, pupa, and adult.

1. A female adult black swallowtail butterfly is laying eggs on a plant. The eggs come from inside her body.

The tiny eggs are pale yellow.

2. A larva **hatches**, or comes out of the egg. The larva is called a caterpillar.

3. The caterpillar makes a case. It is now a pupa.

4. The pupa changes into a beautiful black swallowtail butterfly. This is the adult stage.

Butterfly eggs

Some butterflies lay one egg under each plant leaf. Some butterflies lay eggs on top of leaves. A giant swallowtail butterfly has laid a bunch of orange eggs on top of this leaf.

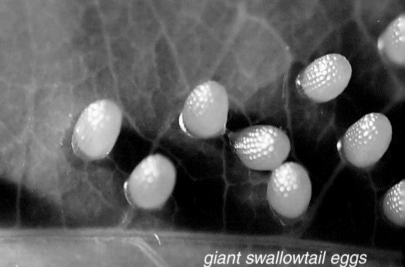

giant swallowtail eggs

This butterfly is laying its eggs under a leaf.

*giant
swallowtail
butterfly*

*This butterfly lays its
white eggs inside the
curled leaves of a plant.*

eggs

The eggs hatch

1. This monarch caterpillar is hatching.

These pictures show an egg laid by a monarch butterfly. A caterpillar has grown inside the egg. After a few days, the caterpillar hatches. It chews its way out of its eggshell. It then eats its eggshell. The eggshell helps the caterpillar grow.

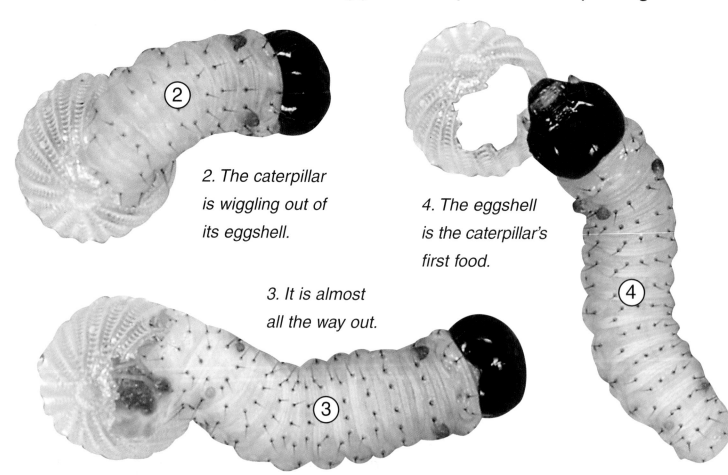

2. The caterpillar is wiggling out of its eggshell.

4. The eggshell is the caterpillar's first food.

3. It is almost all the way out.

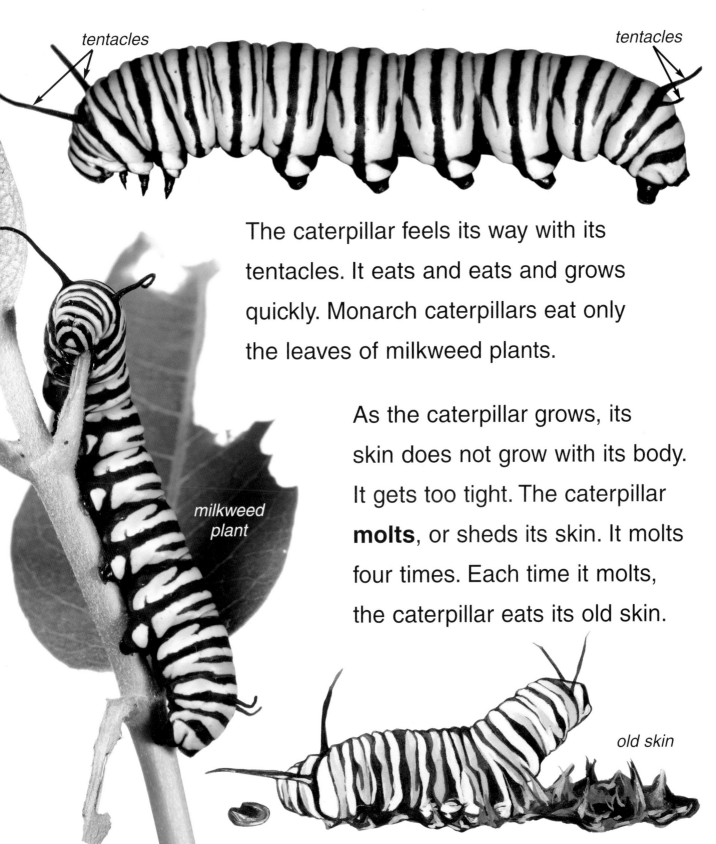

tentacles

tentacles

The caterpillar feels its way with its tentacles. It eats and eats and grows quickly. Monarch caterpillars eat only the leaves of milkweed plants.

As the caterpillar grows, its skin does not grow with its body. It gets too tight. The caterpillar **molts**, or sheds its skin. It molts four times. Each time it molts, the caterpillar eats its old skin.

milkweed plant

old skin

Caterpillar bodies

Caterpillar bodies are very different from butterfly bodies. A butterfly has six legs, but a caterpillar has many more legs! Only the first six legs of a caterpillar are **true legs**. They are joined to the caterpillar's thorax. The other ten legs are just stumps called **prolegs**. Prolegs help a caterpillar climb and hang on to plants. The prolegs are on a caterpillar's abdomen.

Someone has put shoes on this caterpillar, but are the shoes on its true legs?

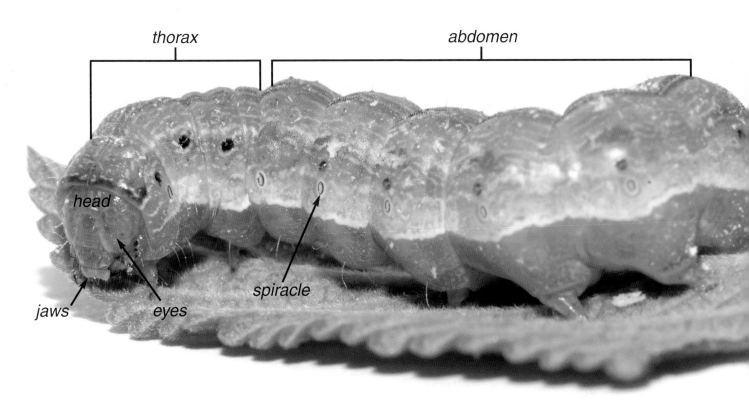

thorax

abdomen

head

jaws

eyes

spiracle

head

spines

tubercle

Caterpillars breathe through tiny holes called **spiracles**. Some caterpillars are covered with **spines**, or stiff hairs. The spines of some caterpillars can cause painful stings, when touched. The spines of this caterpillar are growing out of small blue knobs called **tubercles**.

Staying safe

Caterpillars do not look anything like butterflies. They do not look like one another, either. Caterpillars can have different shapes and colors. They also have different **patterns** on their bodies. Patterns are made up of colors or shapes that repeat. Colors, shapes, and patterns help caterpillars hide from **predators**. Predators are animals that eat other animals.

eyespots

Does this caterpillar have big eyes? No, it has **eyespots**. Eyespots are not real eyes. They are patterns that make caterpillars look bigger and scarier to predators.

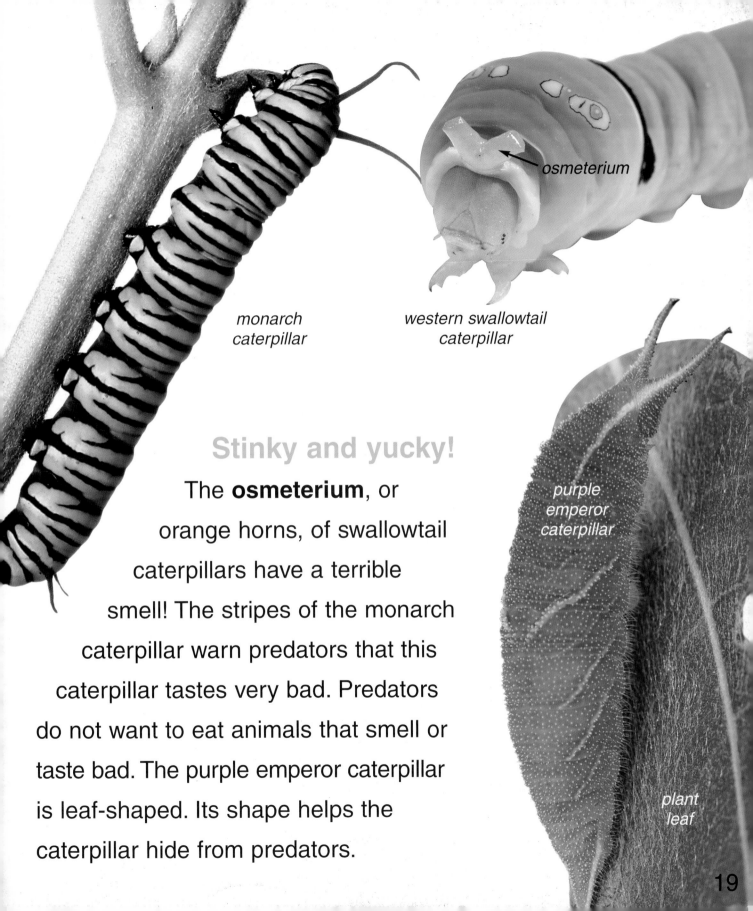

monarch
caterpillar

osmeterium

western swallowtail
caterpillar

*purple
emperor
caterpillar*

Stinky and yucky!

The **osmeterium**, or
orange horns, of swallowtail
caterpillars have a terrible
smell! The stripes of the monarch
caterpillar warn predators that this
caterpillar tastes very bad. Predators
do not want to eat animals that smell or
taste bad. The purple emperor caterpillar
is leaf-shaped. Its shape helps the
caterpillar hide from predators.

*plant
leaf*

① ② ③

chrysalis

Big changes

The caterpillar grows and molts four times. Then it finds a place to hang and molts one last time. These pictures show a monarch caterpillar becoming a pupa and then a butterfly.

1. First, the caterpillar turns its head from side to side to spin some **silk**. It attaches a silk **button** to the branch.
2. The caterpillar hangs from the button and molts.
3. A hard case, called a **chrysalis**, forms around its body. Inside the case, the caterpillar turns to liquid.

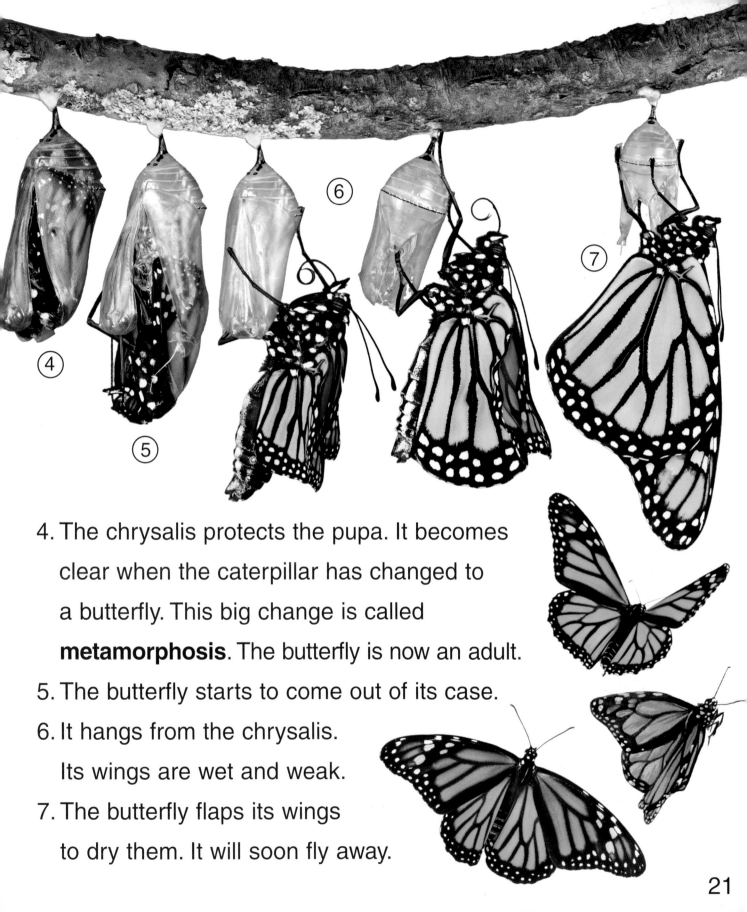

④

⑤

⑥

⑦

4. The chrysalis protects the pupa. It becomes clear when the caterpillar has changed to a butterfly. This big change is called **metamorphosis**. The butterfly is now an adult.

5. The butterfly starts to come out of its case.

6. It hangs from the chrysalis. Its wings are wet and weak.

7. The butterfly flaps its wings to dry them. It will soon fly away.

Match them up!

Each caterpillar on this page will become a butterfly or moth shown on the next page. Have fun matching the right pairs!

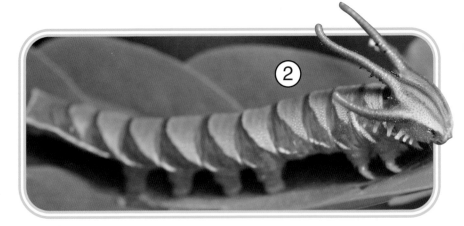

plain Nawab butterfly

peacock butterfly

Answers:

1. peacock butterfly
2. plain Nawab butterfly
3. monarch butterfly
4. luna moth
5. Sammy swallowtail

Sammy swallowtail

monarch butterfly

luna moth

23

Words to Know and Index

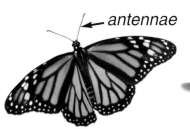

antennae

adults
pages 10, 11, 21

caterpillars
pages 11, 14, 15, 16, 17, 18, 19, 20, 21, 22

chrysalis
pages 20, 21

eggs (hatching)
pages 10, 11, 12–13, 14

food
pages 5, 9, 14, 15

life cycle
pages 10–11, 20–21

molting
pages 15, 20

egg hatching

moths
pages 8–9, 22, 23

pupa
pages 10, 11, 20, 21

wings
pages 4, 7, 8, 9, 21

scales